BUILDING JEWISH LIFE
Ḥanukkah

by Joel Lurie Grishaver

photographs by Jane Golub, Joel Lurie Grishaver
and Alan Rowe

illustrated by Joel Lurie Grishaver
additional line art by Jonathan D. Smith

Torah Aura Productions
Los Angeles, California

For the Hevra which is CAJE

Israel needs modern Hasmoneans, not to draw their swords and shed their blood upon the field of battle, but to save Israel from ignorance, its greatest enemy.

Samson S. Benderly

*

Thank You:
Temple Beth El, San Pedro
Temple Emanuel, Beverly Hills
Shir Hadash—The New Reform Congregation, Encino
Brett and Brian Willis
Daniel Huberman
David Passman
Third Grade Class of Temple Beth El, San Pedro
Barbara Trager
Robin Herwitt
Melton Research Center

Our Advisory Committee:
Melanie Berman, Sherry Bissel-Blumberg, Gail Dorph, Paul Flexner, Dr. Emanuel Gold, Frieda Huberman, Ben Zion Kogen, Debi Mahrer, Fran Pearlman, Peninnah Schram, Joyce Seglin.

Our contributors
illustrations for *The Return of the Junkyard Menorah*
© Jonathan D. Smith

Our Professional Services:
copyeditor: Carolyn Moore-Mooso
Alef Type & Design
Alan's Custom Lab
Gibbons Color Lab
West Coast Graphics
Delta Lithograph

ISBN 0-933873-13-1

Library of Congress Catalog Card Number 87-040233

Torah Aura Productions
4423 Fruitland Avenue
Los Angeles, California 90058

Manufactured in the United States of America.

PART ONE: WHAT WE DO ON ḤANUKKAH

Winter is the season when the days are short and cold. In winter it gets dark very early. We have long, dark nights and very short days.

Ḥanukkah is a holiday which happens in the middle of winter. It is a holiday which takes place on some of the shortest, coldest, darkest days of the year.

On Ḥanukkah we learn that even when things seem darkest, there is always light.

This is a *Hanuk-ki-ah*. It is also called a Ḥanukkah menorah. It holds the lights of Ḥanukkah.

Ḥanukkah is a holiday which lasts for eight days. On the first night we light one candle. We light two candles on the second night. Every night we add another candle.

When we light our Ḥanuk-ki-ah we become part of the story of Ḥanukkah.

Hanukkah means "dedication." When a new building or bridge is opened for the first time, there is often a big event called a "dedication."

Hanukkah is a yearly way of remembering when the Maccabees **rededicated** the Temple in Jerusalem. When the Temple in Jerusalem was turned into a place where Greek idols were worshiped, the Maccabees fought back. They won a war, cleaned up the Temple, and threw out all the Greek idols. Then they lit the Great Menorah.

A dedication is a way of announcing how a building or bridge should be used. When the Maccabees rededicated the Temple, they again made it a place to worship the One God. When we light the Hanuk-ki-ah, we too, make a dedication.

This is a *dreidle*. In Hebrew it is called a *se-vi-von*. We use the dreidle to play a game. The dreidle has four sides. Each side has a Hebrew letter on it: **Nun, Gimmel, Hey,** and **Shin**.

When the dreidle lands on **Nun**, you get "*nichts*," nothing.

When the dreidle lands on **Gimmel**, you get "*ganz*," everything.

When the dreidle lands on **Hey**, you get "*halb*," half.

When the dreidle lands on **Shin**, you have to "*shtel*," put in.

Dreidle is more than a game. The *sevivon* also teaches an important lesson.

The words *nichts, ganz, halb,* and *shtel* are in Yiddish. It is a special Jewish language made up of Hebrew, German and lots of other languages. Yiddish is spoken by Jews from Eastern Europe.

The four Hebrew letters שׁ ה ג נ **Nun, Gimmel, Hey,** and **Shin** also stand for four Hebrew words.

נֵס גָּדוֹל הָיָה שָׁם

Nes Gadol Hayah Sham.
A great miracle happened there.

The story of Ḥanukkah is the story of a miracle. It is the story of finding light when everything seemed to be dark and black.

Ḥanukkah is a fun holiday. It is a time for games and parties, for giving gifts, for eating potato latkes, and for having a good time. On Ḥanukkah we are proud to be Jews.

On Ḥanukkah the big *mitzvah* is lighting and saying the blessing over the Ḥanukkah lights.

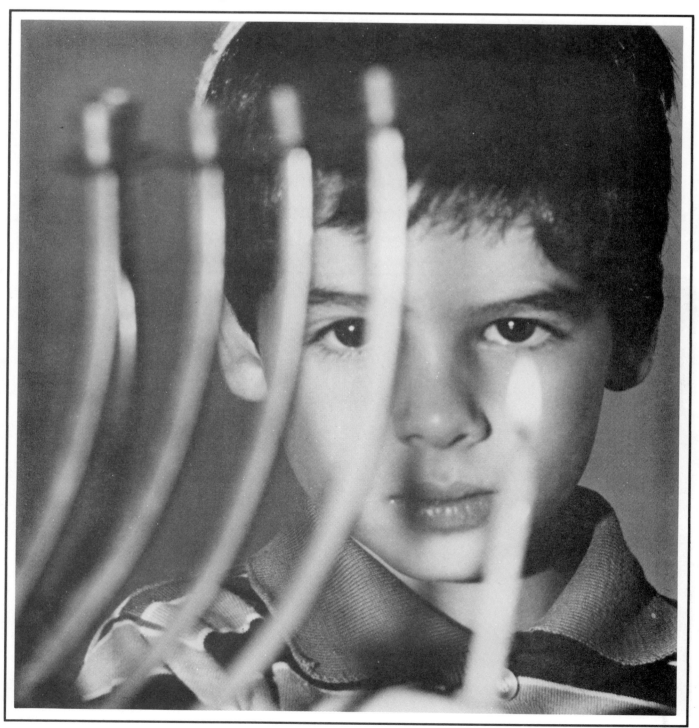

When we light the Hanuk-ki-ah we are doing the same thing the Maccabees did 2,000 years ago.

When we look into the flames, we remember their story. We think about how brave they were, and try to see how we, too, can be Maccabees in our own way.

PART TWO: THE STORY OF ḤANUKKAH

The first Ḥanukkah was a long time ago. In happened after all the stories in the Bible had already taken place, but long before Columbus discovered America. It happened 165 years before the year One.

The important people in the Ḥanukkah story are:

Mattathias, a Kohein who started the Maccabees.

Judah, Mattathias' son who led the Maccabees.

Antiochus IV, a wicked emperor of Syria.

Discuss:
Why is it important to study a story which took place so long ago?
Why is it important to remember about the Maccabees?

We also have:

The Syrian Army

The Jews who want to do Jewish things

The Jews who want to be like the Greeks

and **The Maccabees.**

Ever since Bible times, Jews had lived in the land of Israel. They farmed their land, followed the Torah, and came three times a year to give thanks to God at the Temple in Jerusalem.

On *Sukkot*, on *Pesaḥ*, and on *Shavuot*, they brought the first and the best of what they grew as gift-offerings. They thanked God for rain, for good fortune, for peace, and for the good health of the people they loved.

Discuss:
Jews no longer have one central Temple in Jerusalem. How do we thank God? How do we ask God for peace, good health and the other things we want?

In the Temple, one family from the tribe of Levi, the family of Aaron, led the services and offered the gifts. Each was a Kohein.

For a long, long time, things stayed the same. Most Jews lived in small villages, worked on their farms, and brought their gift-offerings to the Temple three times a year.

Things started to change when the Greeks sent out armies to conquer the world. Everywhere the Greek army went, they brought Greek things. Every time they took over a country they brought Greek sports, Greek music, Greek theater, Greek science, Greek books and the worship of many Greek gods.

When the Greeks came to the land of Israel, they called the country "Judea." They made Jerusalem into a Greek city. They built all kinds of Greek places.

There were theaters where Greek plays were performed, libraries where Greek books could be read, gymnasia where Greek sports could be played, and temples where the idols of Greek gods could be worshiped.

The Greeks didn't make Jews do Greek things. They also didn't stop Jews from doing Jewish things. They thought that plays, athletics, science, and even the worship of their many gods were gifts to the people they conquered. As long as they paid their taxes, Jews were free to choose.

Some Jews really liked being like the Greeks. They began to wear Greek clothing, give their children Greek names, and join in all the new Greek activities.

Other Jews chose to spend their time doing Jewish things, and protecting the customs and teachings of the Jewish tradition.

Discuss:
1. How is our life like the life of the Jews who lived in those days?
2. What Greek things do we do? What Jewish things do we do?

Most of the time, being a Greek was lots of fun. Most Greek things were things which made you feel good. Going to a play, working out at the gym, or learning a new idea were all fun. Being a Greek meant working hard to have a good time.

Being a Jew was fun, too, but it was different. Jewish activities like Shabbat, studying Torah, and giving *tzedakah* were things which brought peace and justice to all people. Being a Jew meant working hard to make the world the best possible place for all people.

There were lots of fights between the Jews who started doing Greek things and the Jews who kept doing Jewish things. Each group wanted all Jews to be like them.

Discuss:
What is the difference between "being like a Greek" and "being a Jew?"

The Greeks conquered countries all over the world. It was a big empire—too big. It broke into many pieces. An emperor of Syria named Antiochus IV took control of Judea.

Antiochus was crazy. He was so crazy that he wanted everyone to think that he was a god. He put idols of himself everywhere. He wanted people to bow down to them, but almost no one did.

Antiochus made the Jews who wanted to be like the Greeks his favorites. He helped them become the bosses of the government of Judea and in charge of the services in the Temple.

The Jews who wanted to do Jewish things were very angry. Judea was becoming too Greek. A Jewish Head Kohein, who wanted Antiochus' help, even gave him some of the holy golden bowls and tools used in the Temple.

One day people began to whisper. There was a rumor. Everyone thought that Antiochus was dead. The Jews who wanted Jerusalem, Judea and the Temple to be more Jewish guessed that this was the right time to fight back. They started a revolution.

It was a mistake. Antiochus wasn't dead. He also wasn't happy that some Jews were fighting against the people he wanted to lead their government and their worship services. He sent his army to stop the revolution.

Discuss:
The Jews who wanted to do Jewish things fought against the Jews who were doing Greek things. When should a person start a fight?

Antiochus also decided to make sure that the Jews who wanted to do Jewish things would never again fight back against the Jews he put in charge. He decided to force all Jews to do Greek things.

Antiochus made doing Jewish things against the law. He made it against the law to celebrate Shabbat, against the law to eat kosher food, and even made it against the law to teach Torah.

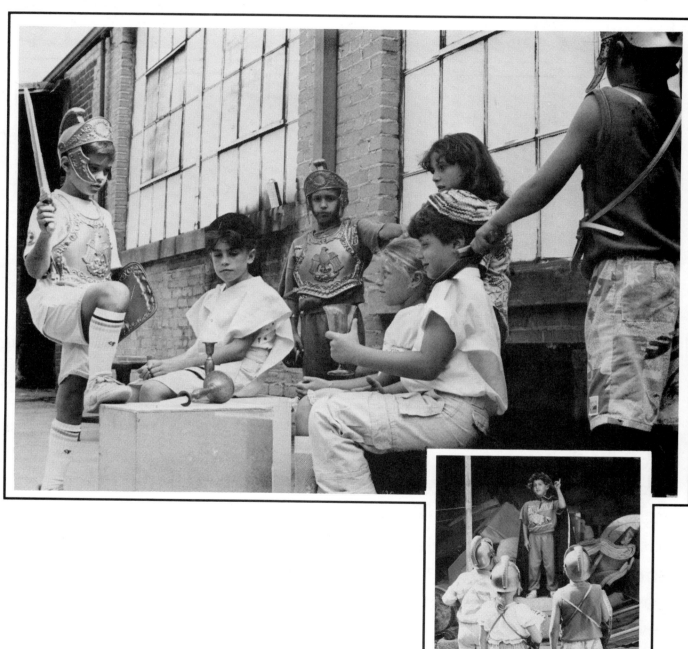

To make sure that no one would ever think there was a future in doing Jewish things, Antiochus turned the Temple in Jerusalem into a place to worship Greek gods. As the final insult, he even had pigs brought into the Temple.

All over Judea, Antiochus' soldiers tried to make Jews stop doing Jewish things and force them to worship Greek gods.

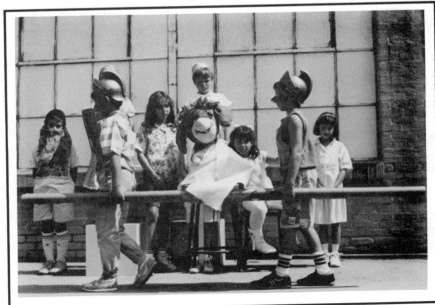

In a little town called Modi'in, the idols were set up and all the town's people were gathered. Syrian soldiers were there to make sure that all the Jews worshiped the Greek god.

When one Jew started to bring a gift-offering to the idol, Mattathias, an old Kohein who lived in Modi'in, took out a hidden sword and killed him. The Syrian soldiers were quickly killed by other Jews.

Mattathias shouted, "Let everyone who believes in following the Torah and keeping the Covenant follow me."

Discuss:
Mattathias fought back, because his freedom to live as a Jew was taken away. To be like him, we should always fight for freedom. Where in the world do people need help winning their freedom?

For more than two years, the Maccabees hid in the mountains, sneaking down to fight the Syrians. Finally, they were strong enough to capture Jerusalem. They entered the city and found that the Temple was a mess. Judah and his followers began to clean the Temple and make it a holy place again. When it was ready, there was a celebration.

WHY THE ḤANUKKAH STORY HAS THREE DIFFERENT ENDINGS

The first Ḥanukkah was almost 2,000 years ago. That is a long time. The story was told and retold. It was taught by parents to their children and then by them to their children. It has been written down many different times and told in many different ways. The three oldest texts tell three very different stories.

Ending 1
A Special Sukkot

Ending 2
The Iron Spears

Ending 3
The Miracle of the Oil

Ending 1

The Maccabees worked hard to clean the Temple. They built a new altar out of new uncut stones, polished the holy bowls and tools, put new loaves of shewbread on the table, and hung the curtains. Then they were ready to celebrate.

It was winter. Sukkot, the holiday when Jewish farmers asked God for rain, was long past. They had missed their chance to celebrate it. Now that the Temple was holy again, each Maccabee took an *etrog* and a *lulav* and made the first Ḥanukkah the special celebration of an extra Sukkot. Sukkot is a holiday which lasts for eight days.

II Maccabees 10.1-8

Ending 2

The Maccabees worked hard to clean the Temple. They built a new altar out of new uncut stones, polished the holy bowls and tools, put new loaves of shewbread on the table, and hung the curtains. Then they were ready to celebrate.

While they were cleaning the Temple, the Maccabees found eight iron spears. They took these spears and stuck them in the ground and filled them with oil. They made these spears into the first Hanukkiah. This made the rededication of the Temple a Festival of Lights.

Pesikta Rabbati 2.1

Ending 3

The Maccabees worked hard to clean the Temple. They built a new altar out of new uncut stones, polished the holy bowls and tools, put new loaves of shewbread on the table, and hung the curtains. Then they were ready to celebrate.

The Maccabees wanted to light the golden Menorah which was kept in the Temple. While they were cleaning the Temple, they found only one small jar of oil. It was only enough to burn for one day. They sent for more oil. But, while they were waiting, a miracle happened. The oil lasted for eight days.

Babylonian Talmud, Shabbat 21b

Making Meaning

We will never know for sure which, if any, of these endings really happened. What we do know, is that each of these three endings to the Ḥanukkah story can teach us one lesson about the meaning of Ḥanukkah. *Finish these sentences and explain the lesson you think each ending teaches.*

Ending 1:

Sukkot is a holiday which comes every year. It celebrates the way that winter always comes after summer. It is a holiday which celebrates how the year is like a circle—going on forever

When the Temple was turned into a place to worship Greek gods most people thought that the Jewish religion would die. By celebrating a special Sukkot the Maccabees taught us_____

_____

Ending 2:

Spears are weapons of war. They are usually used to kill and destroy.

When the Maccabees came to clean the Temple, they saw that eight iron spears could be turned into a Menorah which gave light. We can learn from what they did that _____

_____

Ending 3:

The oil should never have been able to burn for eight days. A small number of Jewish farmers should never have been able to defeat the great Syrian army.

Somehow the oil did last. Somehow the Maccabees did win. From this we can learn _____

All of these endings teach us that even when things seem darkest, there is always light.

Here are the basic rules for lighting a Ḥanuk-ki-ah:

1. The shamash should always be the highest light. Light it first, then say all the blessings.
2. Always put the candles in on the right-hand side of the menorah.
3. Always light the "new" candle first each light. Light the candles starting on the left-hand side.

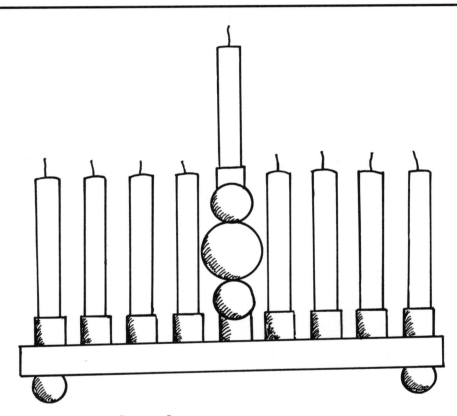

A. Color the shamash red:
B. Color blue the candle lit first on the first night.
C. Color green the candle lit first on the second night.
D. Color pink the candle lit first on the third night.
E. Color purple the candle lit first on the fourth night.
F. Color orange the candle lit first on the fifth night.
G. Color brown the candle lit first on the sixth night.
H. Color light blue the candle lit first on the seventh night.
I. Leave white the candle lit first on the eighth night.

Number these boxes in the right order to tell the story of Ḥanukkah.

☐ The Jews who want to do Jewish things fight back.

☐ Mattathias starts the Maccabees.

☐ Some Jews do Greek things.

☐ Antiochus makes the Jews who do Greek things the bosses.

☐ The Greeks conquer Judea.

☐ Judah becomes the leader.

☐ Antiochus makes doing Jewish things against the Law.

☐ The Maccabees clean the Temple.

A HOME ḤANUKKAH

Match each of these things with the object in their dedication:

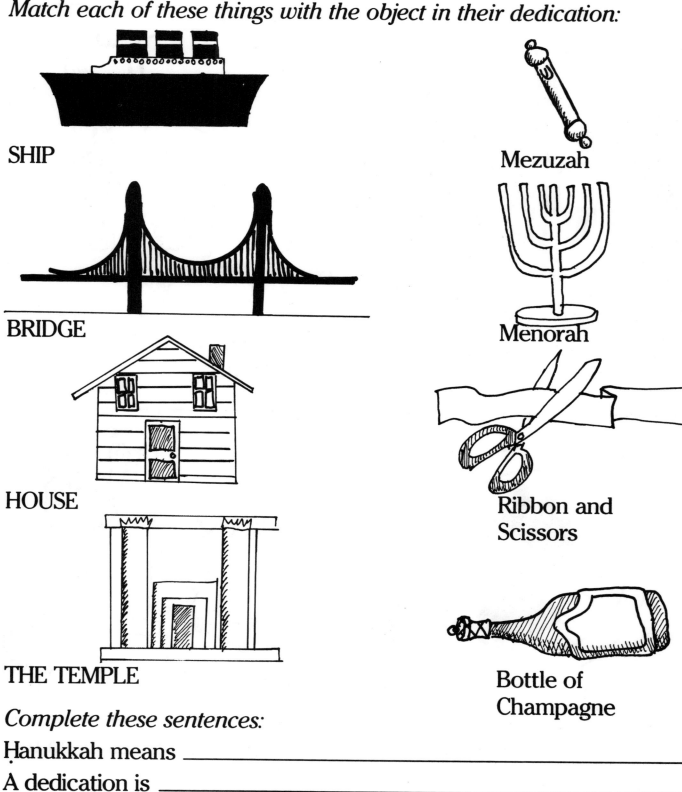

SHIP

Mezuzah

BRIDGE

Menorah

HOUSE

Ribbon and
Scissors

THE TEMPLE

Bottle of
Champagne

Complete these sentences:

Ḥanukkah means _____

A dedication is _____

A JEWISH HOME

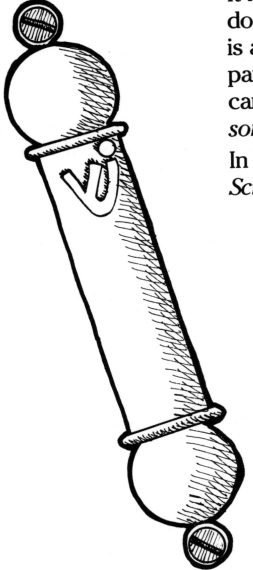

It is a *mitzvah* to put a *Mezuzah* on the doorpost of a Jewish house. In the Mezuzah is a parchment with the Shema and other parts of the Torah. This parchment is carefully hand lettered by a person called a *sofer.*

In his book, *Sofer: The Story of a Torah Scroll,* Eric Ray writes:

> Today when we nail a Mezuzah to the doorpost of our house, apartment or condominium, we still want to protect the place where we live and show that it is a Jewish home.

> A Jewish house is a place where people have respect for all human beings. It is a place where human life is valued and where people believe in treating others with loving concern. It is a holy home, not just a noisy place where no one has feelings for anyone else. A Mezuzah is a reminder that God is part of our family life.

The ceremony for dedicating a Jewish home is nailing up a Mezuzah. It is called a *ḥannukat ha-bayit,* a "House-Ḥanukkah." Name three things which make your house a Jewish place.

1. _____

2. _____

3. _____

The Return of the Junkyard Menorah
or
How Judi learned that it is important to be different

1

My name is Judi and this story is all about how my father and I had a big fight one Ḥanukkah. It happened two years ago when I was almost eight. It is the story of how I learned that it is sometimes important to be different. It is also when Josh became my friend and when we went hunting in the garbage dump.

I was the only Jewish kid in my class at school. A year ago Robert Gotlieb moved into our neighborhood. That now makes two. We go to a synagogue that is more than twenty minutes away. In my Hebrew School class everyone is Jewish.

Every year I hate December. Every year I have to stand up in front of my whole class, sing "I have a little dreidle," and explain about the Maccabees. Everyone looks at me like I'm weird. I hate feeling different. For a long time I didn't understand why we were the only family who celebrated Ḥanukkah. I wanted to be just like everyone else.

2

This is how this story happened. I didn't want to go to school and make a fool of myself talking about Ḥanukkah. The kids in my class weren't interested. Two weeks before winter vacation, I told my father that I wouldn't take the family Ḥanukkiah to school. He said, "You should be proud to be a Jew." That was easy for him to say. He didn't have to stand in front of the classroom and dodge the spitballs that Brian Conroy shoots. Then my father told me the family menorah story again. He told me how my Great-Great-Grandmother Rosenberg brought the family Ḥanukkah Menorah from a place called Bavaria. I don't really know where that is. The rest of the story tells how my Great-Great-Grandmother then took it from Baltimore to San Francisco in her hatbox. It had to travel on boats, trains, and even a covered wagon. It was a good story, but I still didn't want to stand up in front of my class.

38

After the big talk, I knew that my father was going to make me take the Ḥanukkiah to school and tell everyone about the Maccabees, anyway. I had a plan. I took the Rosenberg menorah off the bookcase and hid it in a cardboard box. I didn't know that Mrs. Kapuchki, our cleaning lady, was going to think the box was garbage.

3

That night, my father came into my room to tuck me in. I was still mad at him, but he wanted to have another long talk. He said, "Jews are different from other people. We don't do everything that everybody else does. We have our own important things. Our holiday is Ḥanukkah and Ḥanukkah is a holiday about being different. When Antiochus wanted the Jews to do everything that everyone else did and not be different, the Maccabees had to fight for their freedom. Ḥanukkah teaches us to remember that Jews are different."

Then he picked me up and hugged me. He said, "I want you to be special and different from everyone else. I love you. When you get older and everyone else does things like smoke or drink or take drugs, I want you to know that you can be different. When everyone else you know forgets to be kind to other people, I want you to be kind. When everyone else is afraid to stand up for what is right, I want you to be the one who leads people to do the right thing. Never forget, you are different and special."

He kissed me, said, "Good night," and turned off the light. I didn't really understand him, but I loved him again.

4

The next day I changed my mind. When I came home from school, I went to get the Ḥanukkiah. I wanted to polish it before I took it to class. Then I saw that it was gone. Mrs. Kapuchki said she had put it outside. I ran out to the alley, but the garbage was gone. The truck had taken it away.

That afternoon I had to go to Hebrew School. It was the first night of Ḥanukkah. I didn't want to go. All I could think about was that the Ḥanukkah menorah which had ridden in the covered wagon was now in the garbage. When Mrs. Hessel took out the Ḥanukkiah and had the class practice the blessings, I ran out of the class crying. Josh ran out after me. He was the high school student who helped our class as an aide. He asked me what was wrong. I told him everything.

5

One minute after the bell had rung, Joshua and I were on our way to the garbage dump. He rode me on his handlebars and we got there with at least an hour to look before dark.

The garbage dump was really yuuucky. There were old shoes filled with rotten tomatoes. Soggy papers were everywhere. I felt like I would never get clean ever again in my life; but we kept on looking.

We looked for an hour, and the sun was setting. I had given up. I said, "It's no use. Let's quit. I'm already in trouble. I'm going to be busted for losing the menorah, I don't want to be docked for the rest of my life for coming home late."

Joshua said, "What's the matter? Don't you believe in miracles?" He turned around, picked up a tin can, and said, "I bet you that this can will land on the menorah."

To this day, I don't know how he did it. I don't think Josh knows either. He threw the can high in the air. It went way up and then came down on top of a big pile. When it hit, a tire rolled off of the pile and crashed into a cardboard box. The box moved. All of a sudden I saw the shamash of my Ḥanukkiah sticking through an egg carton. We both ran.

I picked up the Ḥanukkiah and kissed it. I knew just how the Maccabees felt when they cleaned the Temple. I didn't know what to say. Joshua reached into his knapsack and took out a box of Ḥanukkah candles. He didn't say anything. He put them in the Menorah, and right there—in the garbage dump—we lit the candles and sang the blessings. I think I cried again.

When he rode me home, Josh pointed to a neon sign. He said, "A Ḥanukkiah is just like that neon sign. That is why we put it in the window. It lets everyone know that as Jews we are proud to be different. For us, the light of Torah is the most important thing in our life."

6

That night, my father and I lit the Ḥanukkah Menorah again, and put it in the window for everyone to see. I told my father that I was proud to be different. I said, "If someone needs help, I will always be the one to help. If something is right and someone must speak up, I will be that person. I am going to be a good Jew."

Later that night, I sneaked out of bed into the kitchen. I spent hours polishing and cleaning the Ḥanukkah. I felt just like the Maccabees. The Ḥanukkiah that Great-Great-Grandmother Rosenberg brought from Bavaria, and which came from Baltimore on a covered wagon was always going to be protected. Late that night, I had my own Ḥanukkah. My Ḥanukkiah had its own dedication.

ANSWER THESE QUESTIONS:

1. Did Mrs. Gomez bring the Ḥanukkiah from Bavaria? YES NO

2. Did Brian Conroy shoot spit balls at Judi? YES NO

3. Was Judi happy to tell her class about the covered wagon? YES NO

4. Was Josh a member of Judi's Hebrew School class? YES NO

5. Should you light a Ḥanukkiah in a secret place? YES NO

6. What does "Ḥanukkah" mean? _____

7. How was Judi's Ḥanukkah story like the first Ḥanukkah? _____

_____

FEELING JEWISH

The Maccabees were Jews who believed that Jews should do Jewish things. They were proud to be Jews. Sometimes we want to be like the Maccabees. Sometimes we feel like Judi and we want to be like everyone else. These are both important feelings to talk about.

Spend some time talking about feeling Jewish. Use these questions as guidelines. Parents should write down both their own answers and those of their children.

Children should ask their parents:

When was one time you were really proud to be a Jew? _____
_____

When was one time that being a Jew made you feel uncomfortable? _____

Parents should ask their children:

When was one time you were really proud to be a Jew? _____
_____

When was one time that being a Jew made you feel uncomfortable? _____

BUILDING JEWISH LIFE

A Partnership

This **Building Jewish Life** curriculum was designed in the belief that the best possible Jewish education happens only when the classroom and the home are linked. These pages are designed to cycle back and forth between those two realms, and to be used as a tool for learning in each. For this material to work most effectively, teacher and parent must assume interlocking roles and share in actualizing Jewish values and expressions. Each will do it in his/her own way. Each will do it with his/her own style. Together, they will reinforce each other, offering the child tangible experience and understanding of a visionary tradition.

Mitzvah Centered

Mitzvot is a word which means "commanded actions" and is used to describe a series of behaviors which Jewish tradition considers obligations. Classical Judaism teaches that the fabric of Jewish life is woven of 613 of these mandated actions. This series is built around the *mitzvot*, but it uses the term somewhat differently. In our day and age, the *authority* behind any "command" or obligation is a matter of personal faith and understanding. Each Jew makes his/her own peace or compromise with the tradition, affording it a place in his/her own life. In our age, the *mitzvot* have become rich opportunities. They are the things which Jews do, the activities by which we bring to life the ethics, insights, and wisdom of our Jewish heritage. Such acts as blessing holiday candles, visiting the sick, making a seder, comforting mourners, feeding the hungry, hearing the Purim *megillah*, studying Torah, educating our children, and fasting on Yom Kippur are all part of the *mitzvah*—Jewish behavior— "opportunity" list. They are actions which, when they engage us, create moments of celebration, insight, and significance. It is through the *mitzvot* that the richness of the Jewish experience makes itself available. Without addressing the "authority" behind the *mitzvot*, and without assuming "obligation," this series will expose the power of many *mitzvah*-actions and advocate their performance based on the benefit they can bring to your family. It does so comfortably, because we know that you will explore this material and make decisions which are meaningful for you and your family.

The Classroom

In the classroom, this volume serves as a textbook. It helps the teacher introduce important objects, practices, personalities and places in Jewish life. It serves as a resource for exploring Jewish values and engages the students in "making meaning" from Jewish sources. The inclusion of both a parent's guide and a teacher's guide at the end of this volume was an intentional act. We felt it was important for parents to fully understand what was being taught in the classroom.

The Home

This material suggests three different levels of home involvement. On the simplest level, it contains a number of parent-child activities which demand your participation. They cannot be completed without your help. None of these are information-centered. The task of teaching names, pronunciations and facts has been left for the classroom. Rather, these are all moments of sharing values and insights or experimenting with the application of that which has been learned in class. They should be wonderful experiences and they call upon you to be a parent interested in his/her child, not a skilled teacher or tutor.

On a second level, much of this material can also be used to provide "read-aloud" experiences at bedtime, or as the basis for family study and discussion at the dinner table. Do not be afraid to "pre-empt" that which will be taught in class, or to "review" that which your child has learned. The more reinforcement, the better.

Finally, and most dramatically, there is the experience of participating in the *mitzvot* described in this book. We strongly urge you to make this a year to "try out" as many of them as possible. Think of them as the field trips and home experiments which will enrich the classroom experience and make it comprehensible.

The Network

The prime focus of this text series is celebration. Celebrations are better when they are shared with friends. New activities and new challenges are easier when they are shared. Familiar activities are also enriched by the presence of others. Many of the congregations which adopt this series will already have a system of Havurot, Jewish Holiday Workshops, or family activities. Others will organize parallel parent education sessions and special events for the families of the students in this program. We also imagine that some families will network with their friends to "try out" some of these *mitzvah*-events. It is our *strong suggestion* that, at least on an event-to-event basis, you connect with other Jewish families to experience some of the celebrations about which your child will be learning.

ḤANUKKAH

ORIGINS

An irony: Hanukkah is both the Jewish holiday most observed in North America, and the one most misunderstood and misinterpreted.

On December 21st, the tilt of the earth's axis creates the longest night and the shortest day of the year—the winter solstice. In ancient times it was a night of fear and trepidation; fear that the sun would go away forever. The solstice night needed to be a turning point; the sun needed to return, otherwise it would be lost forever. To the primitive mind worship was a form of insurance; gods needed to be reminded and nature needed to be encouraged. When fields needed rain, water was poured onto them and the appropriate gods were asked to imitate the action, much as a young boy is asked to imitate the trickle of the faucet into the bath tub. In the same way, on the shortest night of the year, bonfires were lit and the world was set ablaze—the sun was signaled to return.

The strange alignment of Christmas and Hanukkah is no coincidence. Both celebrations are imprinted on the experience of this ancient watch-night, on waiting for the sun to return. Both celebrations involve the lighting of night fires, and both metaphorically deal with the return of light. It is there, however, that the relationship ends. Hanukkah is not the Jewish Christmas. Its message is the assertive struggle for individuality, not the beginning of universal peace. The seasonal conjunction often is assumed to denote a commonality, when in fact, the analogy to Christmas has both distorted and reconceptualized the Jewish Festival of Lights.

The True Story of Ḥanukkah

While conventional wisdom teaches us to think of Hanukkah as the historic memory of a revolution fought for religious freedom, a kind of Mattathias Washington and the Colonial Maccabees, in truth, Hanukkah commemorates a civil war. It is a conflict rooted in the meaning of being Jewish. This war between Jewish factions was the result of differing reactions to the influx of Greek culture brought by the conquests of Alexander the Great (circa 350 BCE).

1

Before the coming of the Greeks, Judea was essentially a country made up of small farming villages. There were only a few cities, which were primarily local marketplaces, as well as one national religious center, Jerusalem. While there had been brief moments of greatness in the era of David and Solomon, the Jewish state was then merely a small "backwater" farming community situated on the main trade route between the Tigris and Euphrates basin (Babylonia) and the Nile Delta (Egypt). In Jerusalem, the national religious cult was maintained by a priestly class, the Kohanim.

2

When Alexander the Great conquered most of the known world, including Judea, he fermented great social and economic change. The coming of "Greek Culture," lead to the expansion of the city and the development of a middle class, both supported by a vastly increased involvement in international trade. One of the greatest changes in this new urban society was the exponential expansion of leisure time. The Greeks were masters of leisure time, and their best work: athletics, theatre, music, art, and even philosophy and science, was designed to fill leisure time. Hanukkah is rooted in a philosophic difference over the proper use of this new found opportunity for recreation.

3

As Greek city-states propagated in Judea, many farmers moved to the big city, became urban craftsmen, and then exhibited a predictable tendency to assimilate "Greek" trends. They began to eat, talk, dress and play in Greek ways. Some farmers, however, moved to the big city, became craftsmen, and then used the new found leisure time to "conserve" the traditions and customs of their people. The *nouveau* Greeks were known as "Hellenizers." They included many of the old Judean aristocracy and quickly moved into political prominence. The new urban "traditionalists" also banded together. They centered their lives around the synagogue, the *bet midrash* (House of Study), and neighborhood fellowship groups—the first havurot. This group of Jews who centered their life around Jewish practice became known as the "Hasidim." They were forerunners of both the Maccabees and the Pharisees.

4

Alexander died a young man and left no heir. Right after his death, his worldwide empire began to shatter. The Middle East was divided between two military families: the Seleucids who ruled from Syria and the Ptolemies who ruled from Egypt.

Judea was in the middle. It was first awarded to the Ptolemies and then later came under Seleucid influence. While these changes had little direct impact on day-to-day life in Judea, they did affect the local political climate.

In particular, the Hellenizers worked their way into control of the priesthood by using access to the wealth of the Temple treasury to influence the Seleucid rulers. While their motivation may well have been political, the response of the Hasidim was religious—anger at the pollution of their way of life.

5

The situation climaxed during the reign of a Seleucid monarch, Antiochus IV. The Seleucid-Ptolemy conflict and the Hellenizer-Hasid conflict merge to incite a war.

In a desire to solidify his Empire, Antiochus deposed the extant Head Kohein, Onias III, and replaced him with a more Hellenistic leader, Jason. Under Jason, the city of Jerusalem was officially established as a Greek *polis* (city state) and renamed "Antiochia." As part of the process, a gymnasium was established and supported by the Kohanim. Just before going to war with the Ptolemies, Antiochus replaced Jason with an even more sympathetic Head Kohein, Menelaus. Menelaus allowed Antiochus to plunder the wealth of the Temple treasury.

All at once, three things came together. First, the removal of sacred gold objects from the Temple was a sacrilegious act which the Hasidim could not tolerate. Second, Jason (probably backed by the Ptolemies) attempted to return to power as the Head Kohein. Third, a rumor of Antiochus' death (probably devised by Antiochus himself) spread through Judea. Angered by the profanation of the Temple, encouraged (ironically) by the return of Jason, and convinced by the rumor that the time was now right, the Hasidim revolted against Menelaus and the Hellenizer ruling class. It was a civil war which Antiochus' troops quickly ended.

6

Antiochus instantly instituted a two-part campaign to destroy the Hasidim. First, he made a number of basic Jewish practices illegal: Shabbat, Torah study, and circumcision were proscribed. Second, he began a campaign to force the local Jewish population to violate Jewish law by publicly eating pork and participating in pagan rites.

It was these edicts which lead Mattathias, a common Kohein living in the rural community of Modi'in, to revolt. His revolt galvanized the militant Hasidim into the military Maccabees. In order to win their civil war with the Hellenizers, the Seleucid army (a.k.a. "The Greeks") also had to be defeated.

7

In a pattern which history has now seen replicated many times, a local peasant "resistance" movement fought an idealistic guerrilla war—defeating a mercenary army far from their home. A study of the Maccabean wars reveals an abundance of courage and commitment as well as innovative use of guerrilla strategy.

The part of the story which is most critical to the celebration of Hanukkah is, of course the rededication of the Temple. It is here, ironically or perhaps logically, that historical sources are most unclear. A number of historical sources give a series of conflicting reports.

The First Book of Maccabees was probably written in Hebrew in Judea around 120 BCE (close to 300 years after the first Hanukkah). It tells us only, *"They also made new holy vessels, and brought the menorah...into the Temple. They burned incense on the altar and kindled the lights on the menorah, and the Temple was filled with light. For eight days they celebrated the dedication of the altar."* In our earliest records, there was no extraordinary form of celebration—and there was no miracle.

The Second Book of Maccabees was originally a Greek work intended for Jewish audiences outside of the Land of Israel. It was also written around the same time as *First Maccabees*. It tells us: *"After purifying the Temple, they made another altar. Then by striking flint, they made new fire and... offered gift-offerings and incense, and kindled the menorah...."* After echoing the information found in *First Maccabees*, *Second Maccabees* adds: *"On the 25th of Kislev, they now purified the Temple. They celebrated joyfully for eight days, just as one does at Sukkot, because at Sukkot time they had spent the holiday living like wild animals in the mountains and caves. That is why they now came with etrog and lulav..."*

Megillat Ta'anit, a rabbinic work written in the first century CE, forbids fasting on the eight days of Hanuk-kah. It, too, makes no mention of extraordinary celebration or of a miracle. Likewise, Josephus in his *Antiquities of the Jews*, written around 95 CE, also tells the story of the rededication of the Temple and the eight-day celebration which resulted—also without mentioning miracles or extraordinary celebrations.

The famous story of "oil which burned for eight days," is first found in the *Babylonian Talmud*, finished around 500 CE, almost 700 years after the first Hanukkah. It tells us, *"they searched and found only one jar of oil with the official seal of the Head Kohein, but which was only enough to burn for one day; yet a miracle occurred, and the menorah burned for eight days..."*

Pesikta Rabbati is a collection of midrashim completed in the Land of Israel in 847 CE—about 1,000 years after the first Hanukkah. It tells yet another story. It says, *"When they (the Maccabees) came into the Temple, they found eight iron spears which they threw into ground and then kindled lights."*

While the "miracle of oil" story found in the Babylonian Talmud is among the most unlikely of the accounts found in historic sources, it is the one which forms the basis for our popular understanding of Hanukkah. Thinking logically, one would expect Hanukkah to be a celebration of military bravery and might, and a chance to thank God for supporting this miraculous victory. Instead, this popular "miracle of oil" story, absent from all but one account, shifts the emphasis away from the battlefield and into the Temple ritual. Dr. Emanuel Gold explains the apparent cover-up of the true nature of Hanukkah as an attempt by the influential rabbis living within the Roman Empire to preserve the peace: "The miracle was not the victory of 'activism' but of a 'little jar of oil.' This successfully defused many a budding activist from going astray. 'Passivist' peaceful accommodation would be preserved."

The Opportunity of Hanukkah

The tradition considers Hanukkah to be a "minor festival." Its celebration was designed to be a minimal event, involving the performance of only two specific mitzvot: the *lighting of the Hanukkiah* and the *recitation of hallel*—a series of psalms sung as a sequence in the synagogue. *The giving of gifts is not a Hanukkah mitzvah. In particular, it is one "custom" which has no legitimate traditional origins. It is*

In our day the activist...has rekindled the light of the Maccabees and restored the meaning and message of Hanukkah...to bring freedom to the oppressed and hope to those who despair.

---

pure (if inspired) imitation. It is certain that had it not been for the conjunction of Hanukkah with Christianity's major annual celebration, it would have drifted in obscurity. Instead, this celestial alignment, accelerated by the North American commercialization of the season, has supercharged the celebration of this minor event. The need to keep up with (and apart from) the Joneses has infused this annual lighting of lights with a series of folk practices and a spectrum of additional meanings. Plainly and simply put, Hanukkah has devolved into the celebration of not being a Christian.

Hanukkah is a holiday whose true epic origins have been covered-over with the fable of a minor-miracle. It is a holiday whose celebration has been mutated by mistaken analogy to a different myth, and one whose prime message is often warped,

over-generalized, and defused. Despite this negative backstory, Hanukkah remains the cyclic Jewish high point for most Jewish children and their parents—and a time rich with opportunity. Like the winter solstice watch-night onto which it was fused, it remains an annual turning point, and a time to find light in the midst of darkness.

The Opportunity to be Different

Pattie Goldin, the creator of the "Holiday Workshop Series" tells an insightful story. One year at Passover, her daughter came home from college and shared the results of a dorm "bull session." Trying to figure out why she hadn't turned to drinking, drugs or carefree sex as had a number of those with whom she grew up, she had come up with only one answer, "Hanukkah." Her reasoning: "When we had to celebrate Hanukkah while everyone else celebrated Christmas, I learned that it was O.K. to be different. I didn't have to do everything that everyone else did." For Pattie, it was justification for years of "eight nights worth of presents," "homemade decorations," and much self-generated fanfare. For us, the story is the key to the values which the celebration of Hanukkah can teach.

For anyone growing up as a Jew, Hanukkah is a boundary issue. Starting right after Thanksgiving, the sudden flood of "Seasons Greetings" draws a line. No matter how secure and how assimilated one may feel, Santa's assault on the senses underlines the fact that Jews are not full partners in the popular culture. We feel different. While the Talmud's "eight nights of oil" was never designed to compete with *Rudolf the Red Nosed Reindeer*, the present cultural conflict is a direct echo of the cultural conflicts with precipitated the first Hanukkah-Christmas choice—is but the most dramatic of the conflicts which force us to chose between Jewish obligations and the opportunities available in the larger culture. It is a contemporary reincarnation of the Maccabee-Hellenizer decision point. Every Jewish child's sense of isolation during the winter season is ironically an innate understanding of Hanukkah's true meaning. Hanukkah is, from its most authentic roots, the celebration of being different.

The Opportunity to Experience Miracles

The Talmud explains the mitzvah of lighting the Hanukkiah as the responsibility to "advertise the miracle." Hanukkah was to be the yearly affirmation that miracles are possible. The Talmudic lawmakers wanted (for reasons understandable in their era) to root the responsibility for miracles in God. That is the message of "oil lasting for eight days." However, it is equally possible to understand the real miracle of Hanukkah as being the end product of faith in God; a miracle of human commitment—proof of what inspired uncompromising dedication can accomplish. Dr. Gold suggests that this second, modern return to an original understanding, has particular relevance: "For the next thousand or more years (after the Talmudic reshaping of Hanukkah) Jews in dire straits in different parts of the world usually chose the 'passivist' route to accommodation and survival. In our day the activist...has rekindled the light of the Maccabees and restored the meaning and message of H.anukkah— that...to bring freedom to the oppressed, and hope to those who despair, we must be 'active' pursuers of our cause. Our 'miracle' will be achieved when the few, the weak and the just, triumph." While the long-burning oil story is an interesting example of divine sleight of hand, Hanukkah provides a more immediate message—that of human potential. Hanukkah is an opportunity to learn that we can work miracles.

The Opportunity of Re-Dedication

Being a child of New England, Hanukkah is always a winter experience for me. The Hanukkiah kindled in my memory is always set against a window covered in frost or condensed moisture. The flickering light both reflects inside and casts its glow on the cold void.

Hanukkah means dedication. The name was first intended in a very literal fashion. It was the name given to the anniversary of the date when the Maccabees rededicated the Sanctuary in the Temple. Hanukkah doesn't commemorate the date of a Maccabee victory or the end of the Maccabean wars. Rather, it is the annual remembrance of a hands-on task, the cleaning and purifying of the national sanctuary. The rededication of the Temple on that first Hanukkah, culminated in the relighting of the golden menorah. When the time came to create an annual event remembering this first dedication, that same culminating act, the lighting of lights, became the central feature.

Like most other Jewish rituals, the kindling of the Hanukkiah is a carefully choreographed event. The tradition carefully prescribes the beginning point and direction (see page 33). In the Talmud, detailed specifications are given as to the kind of oil and wick which may be used. Also found in the Babylonian Talmud, is the description of a three-tiered fulfillment of this mitzvah. In Shabbat 21b ff., we are given the sense of a different kind of dedication.

1. *The basic mitzvah of Hanukkah requires each family to light one light (candle) per night.*
2. *Those who really want to fulfill this mitzvah should light one light for each family member each night.*
3. *To completely fulfill this mitzvah, a person should light 36 candles during Hanukkah. There are two opinions about the proper sequence.*
   Bet Shammai taught: "One should light eight candles on the first night, and one less each following night."
   Bet Hillel taught: "One should light one candle on the first night, and one more each following night."

Today, common practice opts for the maximal fulfillment of this mitzvah as understood by the school of Hillel. In the Jerusalem Talmud, Rabbi Yose ben Zabida explains this practice, "One should ascend in matters of holiness and not descend." This is the key to another understanding of dedication.

Making a dedication is making a commitment. A dedication is a life choice, the affirmation of a sense of direction. The physical dedication of the Temple by the Maccabees was the culmination of a life commitment. The annual enactment of that event calls upon each of us to make our own dedications and reaffirm the vectors which guide our own life. Gazing into the Hanukkah lights, we are called upon to be Maccabees and to reestablish the things in our lives that are significant enough to fight over. We are called upon to make a maximal dedication, to ascend and not descend. Gazing into the Hanukkah lights, we see an inside reflection and cast a glow through the frost into the cold void.

The Lighting of Hanukkah Lights

Candles are hypnotic. The collected blaze of the Hanukkiah invites reflection. When we look into the flames, we remember more than we know, and feel more than we can express. Flames work that way.

The official procedure for lighting of the Hanukkah lights calls for the recitation of three brakhot. Together these three blessings guide our understanding of this celebration.

The first blessing is the *birkat mitzvah*. It follows the familiar formula "who made us holy with the mitzvot, and made it a mitzvah for us to..." Mitzvot are preceded or followed by a brakhah using this formula. It focuses our attention and defines the action as one which will lead to meaning.

The second blessing is *she'asah nissim la'avoteinu*. It connects our actions on each night of Hanukkah to those of the first Hanukkah. It states, "who performed miracles for our ancestors, in those days at this time of year." We connect our present actions to our people's history. We reflect on our own understanding of miracles. In reenacting the first Hanukkah, we search for its meaning.

The third blessing is the *she-he-heyanu*. It is said only on the first night of Hanukkah and at the beginning of most special Jewish events. It thanks God "for giving us life, sustaining us, and helping us to reach this moment." It sets the moment apart as a special time.

Rituals mean more than we can explain. In lighting the Hanukkiah we conjure our memories of the Maccabees, of the first Hanukkah, of the meaning of dedication. Even without full explanations and even without firm conclusions, we make rituals part of who we are. The Hebrew phrases lead us to gaze into the flames and reflect. To fully understand Hanukkah, just watch your children watching their candles.

Hanukkah is the single event which unifies the greatest number of Jews. Its history and its temporal nexus fill it with meaning. It is a moment rich in opportunity.

FOR THE TEACHER

The Ḥanukkah volume of **Building Jewish Life** centers on three objectives:
1. Students will master the basic vocabulary of Ḥanukkah, consisting of the words listed in the Essential Vocabulary section below.
2. Students will read about, discuss and be able to tell the story of Ḥanukkah, including identifying Antiochus, Mattathias, Judah, the Syrian Army, and the Maccabees, and will participate in a discussion of the three different endings to the Ḥanukkah story.
3. Students will learn about, practice, be able to explain and participate in the lighting of the Hanuk-ki-ah and in the playing of dreidle.

ESSENTIAL VOCABULARY

Hanuk-ki-ah	A lamp stand with nine flames used to celebrate Ḥanukkah.
Menorah	The Hebrew word for "lamp" which usually refers to the 7 branched lamp stand which was found in the Temple.
Hanukkah	A Hebrew word which means, "dedication" which is the name of the holiday which commemorates when the Maccabees rededicated the Temple.
Dreidle	Yiddish name for the four-sided top used to play a Ḥanukkah game.
Se-vi-von	Hebrew name for this four-sided top.
Nes Gadol Hayah Sham	"A great miracle happened there." The message found in the four letters on the dreidle.

We assume that this material will cover three classroom sessions. Teachers should feel free to adapt and improvise according to (1) time available, (2) age and ability of students, (3) involvement of families, (4) previous background, and (5) moments of inspiration.

LESSON ONE
An Ever-Burning Light

1. SET INDUCTION: CLUSTER your class in a dark area and LIGHT one candle. Have everyone LOOK at the flame, and DISCUSS why people like to look at candles. Then EXPLAIN that in our synagogue there is a NER TAMID, an ever-burning light. It is a flame which never goes out. ASK: "What does it teach us?" ACCEPT all answers. ESTABLISH: "It reminds us that God is always with us."

LIGHT a Hanuk-ki-ah. Do not say the blessings. ASK students to identify the object. BRAINSTORM everything they already know about Ḥanukkah and its story. CONCLUDE: "Hanukkah is a holiday which remembers when the Maccabees kept the ever-burning light in the Temple from going out. Today we are going to learn their story."

2. READING THE HANUKKAH STORY: Have your students OPEN this book together to page 10. READ together the story of Ḥanukkah. STOP along the way to (a) check for comprehension, (b) discuss some of the questions at the bottom, and (c) to allow for student questions.

STOP BEFORE page 26. ASK three students: "When you go home and your parents ask, 'What happened in class today?'—what will you tell them? If you pick properly, you should get three very different answers. POINT OUT: All three of these students were in the same class. They took part in the same lesson, yet they tell very different things about it. The same is true of the Ḥanukkah story.

READ and discuss the last part of the story. FINISH with page 30. DO the Making Meaning exercise as a class, then allow individuals time to write their own answers down.

3. PLAYING "WHAT'S MY LINE": Before class WRITE seven one paragraph biographies of Antiochus, Mattathias, Judah, The Syrian Army, The Jews who did Greek things, the Jews who did Jewish things, and the Maccabees. Each one should begin, "I am a ....." and not contain the name of the person(s). PASS these out to six students. Have the rest of the class open their books to pages 10-11. ASK the students with the biographies to read them one at a time, and ask the rest of the students to GUESS who they are. ASSIGN students to reread the Ḥanukkah story and complete pages 34-35 as homework.

4. PRACTICING THE BRAKHOT: DEMONSTRATE the right way to light the Hanuk-ki-ah (see pages 32-33). TEACH and/or PRACTICE the brakhot.

5. CLOSURE: GATHER the class around the lighted Hanuk-ki-ah. LOOK into the flames together. DISCUSS: "When you look at the lighted Hanuk-ki-ah—what do you think about?"

LESSON TWO
The meaning of Dedication

1. PRACTICING LIGHTING THE HANUK-KI-AH: Bring 3 or 4 Hanuk-ki-ot to class. Have at least 5 candles for each one. DEMONSTRATE the correct way to light the Hanuk-ki-ah. (See page 33). Then DIVIDE the class into groups. Ask the group the place the right number of candles in the right places for the third night of Ḥanukkah. Then RECITE the brakhot together while they PANTOMIME the lighting. REPEAT for the first and fourth nights.

2. SET INDUCTION ON DEDICATION: ASK: "Imagine that this congregation built a new sanctuary (place where we pray). What should be done on the first day that the building can be used?" ACCEPT all answers. INTRODUCE the word "dedication." Together, READ the first part of this book, pages 3-9.

3. REVIEWING THE STORY OF HANUKKAH: EXPLAIN: "Hanukkah means "dedication." ASK: "How is Ḥanukkah the story of a dedication?" In the process of answering the question, REVIEW the whole Ḥanukkah story. Have the class COMPLETE the exercise on page 36. Assign them to complete page 37 with their parents as homework.

4. ACTING THE STORY OUT: PICK students to improvise the following scenes in front of the class: (a) Greeks show the Jews all the "gifts they are bringing." (b) An argument between Jews who want to do Greek things and Jews who want to do only Jewish things. (c) Antiochus ordering the Jews not to do Jewish things (and having his soldiers mess up the Temple). (d) Mattathias fighting back. (e) Jews cleaning up the Temple and celebrating the first Ḥanukkah. DISCUSS each scene before it is acted out. AFTER each performance, let the audience make suggestions and then let the actors try it again.

5. PLAYING DREIDLE: REVIEW the rules for playing dreidle. BREAK the class up into small groups. ALLOW them time to play together.

LESSON THREE
A Family Celebration

0. INVITE PARENTS: SEND invitations home, invite parents to join your class celebration. ASK each family to bring a Hanuk-ki-ah to class.

1. WELCOMING PARENTS: DIVIDE the whole group into five teams of families. ASSIGN each family to write a 3-minute play on one of these five scenes. (These are the same ones rehearsed with the kids in the previous class. (a) Greeks show the Jews all the "gifts they are bringing." (b) An argument between Jew who want to do Greek things and Jews who want to do only Jewish things. (c) Antiochus ordering the Jews not to do Jewish things (and having his soldiers mess up the Temple). (d) Mattathias fighting back. (e) Jews cleaning up the Temple and celebrating the first Ḥanukkah.

2. PRESENTING THE PLAYS: Have the groups present the scenes. Provide the transitional narration.

3. THREE STATIONS: SET up three learning stations: Making Latkes, Reading and discussing the story: **The Return of the Junkyard Menorah** and Playing dreidle. ROTATE families between these three experiences.

4. DOING/PRACTICING THE BRAKHOT: ASK each family to light their own Hanuk-ki-ah. RECITE the Brakhot together. Then join in singing your favorite Ḥanukkah songs.